Original title:
Laughing at the Big Questions

Copyright © 2025 Creative Arts Management OÜ
All rights reserved.

Author: Evan Hawthorne
ISBN HARDBACK: 978-1-80566-042-2
ISBN PAPERBACK: 978-1-80566-337-9

Giggling at the Infinite

In a universe so vast and wide,
We ponder life with eyes open wide.
Is there purpose in the stars' bright glow?
Or just a cosmic joke we don't yet know?

Why do socks, when paired, still disappear?
Do they escape to realms far and near?
While we question where they might roam,
They giggle, saying, "This is our home!"

Do ducks quack in a universal tone?
Or do they sing to the seeds they've sown?
As they waddle with such flair and pride,
We chuckle at what they might confide.

What if trees could share their dreams at night?
Would they whisper tales in soft moonlight?
Saying, "We root for you, rise up tall!"
As leaves dance, they hear our call.

With questions swirling, let's take a seat,
For pondering life can be quite a treat.
In this grand joke, we play our part,
With laughter echoing in each heart.

Whispers in the Cosmic Wind

In a grand dance of stars so bright,
The universe chuckles, full of delight.
Planets spin tales in a cosmic breeze,
Silly secrets shared amongst the trees.

A comet zips past with a wink and a grin,
Who knows which mystery lies within?
Black holes with their secrets, yet to unfold,
Whispering laughter that never grows old.

The Riddles of the Infinite

Why does the cosmos seem so vast?
Yet, it spins its tales, ever fast.
Each riddle wrapped in a nebula's glow,
Makes us wonder what we really know.

Stars giggle softly, as they twinkle clear,
Creating questions that dance in our ear.
A puzzle here, a riddle there,
The infinite asks with a playful flair.

Giggles Beneath the Stars

Under a blanket of shimmering night,
We share our dreams, our laughter so light.
The moon winks down, with a cheeky grin,
As we ponder the places that we've all been.

Galaxies swirl, but they don't take a frown,
Instead, they twirl in a merry-go-round.
Each twinkling star shares a chuckle or two,
As they glimpse the Earth and all we pursue.

Cosmic Laughter

In the depths of space where silence should reign,
Echoes of laughter ripple like rain.
Every supernova bursts with a cheer,
Exploding with joy, its message is clear.

We dance with the quarks in a jest so divine,
What makes us human is a fragile design.
Yet the galaxies giggle, they tease and they play,
Turning big questions to humor each day.

Life's Mysteries

As we explore what it means to be wise,
The universe grins in a thousand disguise.
With every answer, it throws us a jest,
It's all in good fun, put our minds to the test.

From atoms to stars, the jokes never cease,
A cosmic comedy that brings us peace.
So we ponder the big stuff with a wink and a grin,
Finding joy in the journey where laughter begins.

The Paradox of Joy and Pain

Joy dances lightly on life's tightrope,
While sorrow trips with a heavy hope.
Laughter echoes through shadows we chase,
As we juggle truth with a smiling face.

In moments of bliss wrapped in despair,
Who knew that joy needed a shifty pair?
With every stumble, a chuckle we share,
Life's an odd joke, if you really dare.

Smiles in the Silence of Space

Among the stars we tiptoe with glee,
Floating past comets, just you and me.
Gravity's just a force pulling us down,
But we wear our smiles like a cosmic crown.

Planets aligned in a cosmic jest,
While aliens giggle, they simply know best.
In this vast void, we find our embrace,
As stardust tickles the edges of space.

The Comedian of Creation

In the beginning, a wink and a grin,
Creation giggled, and let the fun begin.
Stars were born like punchlines in light,
While planets spun stories, day into night.

From tiny atoms to galaxies wide,
The universe chuckles, no reason to hide.
Every quark a punchline, every black hole a laugh,
As we ride this wild, cosmic craft.

Quips from the Quasar

A quasar beams with jokes from afar,
Its light a shimmering, hilarious bazaar.
Echoes of laughter stretch light-years ahead,
As cosmic giggles fill the void instead.

Each photon whispers a quirky refrain,
Turning dark matter into silly gain.
From the vastness of space, we're never alone,
In the cosmic comedy, we've all grown.

Grins in the Gaps of Understanding

When pondering the cosmic view,
Do stars giggle at what we do?
A quasar winks, a comet sighs,
As we chase truths in our whys.

Our brains are puzzled, minds a whirl,
Yet life's a dance, a funny twirl.
So take a step, embrace the jest,
In the big unknown, we're all a mess.

The Lightness of Life's Questions

What's the purpose, where's the aim?
Like ducks on water, it's all a game.
Each query floats, a feathered dream,
While wisdom tricks, a playful scheme.

We seek the meaning, hunt for gold,
But truth just laughs, it's never told.
So while we search, let's skip and hop,
For in the lightness, we'll never stop.

Smirks Through the Wormholes

In wormholes short, our thoughts collapse,
Are we just echoes, or clever taps?
The universe chuckles, stars align,
While we sip tea, lost in time's design.

Did we invent fate, or is it fate's art?
Each question's a puzzle, a quirky part.
With grins ablaze, we sail through queries,
In the cosmos' dance, we cast our theories.

Banter with the Infinite

Oh, clever cosmos, your secrets known,
Yet we ask riddles like seeds that are sown.
In banter bright, we trade a jest,
While time unfolds, a cosmic quest.

With giggles shared in the void that glows,
The universe nods as curiosity grows.
So let's embrace this wild charade,
In humor's arms, our fears will fade.

Puns Across the Panorama

In the sky, big wonders float,
Do fish wear glasses? Let them gloat!
Why did the moon refuse to glow?
It lost its light, put on a show.

A cat's great task? To catch a dream,
With all the mice, it's quite a scheme.
When clouds grab hats and start to dance,
Who knew the sky enjoyed romance?

The mountains giggle in the breeze,
While rivers rush with carefree tease.
Do trees whisper secrets to the night?
They do, but only if it feels right.

So pluck a star or poke a sun,
In the cosmic giggle, we all run.
Big questions float, a funny sight,
Who knew the world was such delight?

Grins Amidst the Grandiosity

Why do elephants never use phones?
They can't find pockets, just big bones.
When planets gossip, what do they say?
"Gas giants look a bit bloated today!"

Why did the comet take a day off?
It felt too fast, began to scoff.
Do black holes have a sense of fun?
They suck us in, but never run.

Stars often argue over their shine,
"Mine is brighter!" "No, it's all mine!"
The universe, a light-filled joke,
But punchlines vanish like a smoke.

So grab a laugh from cosmic plans,
Tickle the stars with your two hands.
In grandeur large, the quirks still gleam,
Where whimsy flows, we dare to dream.

Melodies of Merriment and Mystery

When raindrops fall, do they sing tunes?
Or is it just dancing by the moons?
A whale's deep hum—its thoughts profound,
Or treble clefs where secrets are found?

Do shadows giggle as they stretch wide?
Do they play hide-and-seek with pride?
What does the sun say to the dawn?
"Hey there, friend! Don't you look drawn?"

A crow caws jokes from a tree's high perch,
While pink clouds blush in the evening search.
When time runs fast, it often slips,
But secrets hide in its fleeting quips.

So let's compose this cosmic song,
With chuckles mingled, the notes are strong.
In melodies where laughter breeds,
The universe tosses only seeds.

The Silliness of Stars

What do constellations do at night?
They play cards—who will win that fight?
With the Milky Way as their bright stage,
They spin their tales, page by page.

Do shooting stars have wishes to keep?
Or are they just prancing, not losing sleep?
A wink from the sky, a twinkle here,
What if the cosmos has a sense of cheer?

The suns hold debates on who's the best,
While comets roam, never take a rest.
Galaxies swirl in a dizzy swirl,
While planets plot a cosmic twirl.

So pop some popcorn, catch the show,
In the silly stars, we all can grow.
For in this vastness, we'll find a jest,
A whimsical dance, the universe's quest.

Mirth Making Sense of Madness

In the whirl of thoughts that twirl,
A cat claims the sun, soft as a pearl.
Why chase shadows when skies are bright?
Ask a squirrel, he'll take flight.

Questions climb like vines on walls,
Echoing laughter, as reason falls.
The world's a riddle wrapped in jest,
Grab a cupcake, skip the quest.

Thoughts say, 'What's life all about?'
While ducks parade with a honking shout.
Keep a straight face and just stroll on,
As jester moons tease at dawn.

In chaos, we find our kicks,
With bouncing thoughts and clever tricks.
When life throws curveballs, don't be shy,
Just spin and dance—oh my, oh my!

Quips from the Cosmic Corner

Stars giggle as they flicker bright,
What's the speed of silly light?
Planets bump, and who takes the blame?
Galaxies chuckle, it's all a game.

As comets race with flares of glee,
We ponder where the socks all flee.
Black holes burp, creating a fuss,
While the universe winks at us.

Aliens ponder, 'To be or not?'
As we ask, 'What's in this pot?'
Life's a joke that's hard to crack,
But hey, let's just sit back, relax.

Out in space, they toast with cheer,
Cosmic pies disappear, we cheer!
With every quirk of the cosmic dance,
We find our steps in a goofy prance.

Glee in the Great Unknown

Waves of wonder crash and roll,
What tickles the heart and feeds the soul?
Lions laugh in the thick old grass,
While cosmic giggles through the ages pass.

Unraveled mysteries in tangled yarn,
Who knew a worm could wear a crown?
In every question, a spark ignites,
Chasing shadows, chasing lights.

Time hops like a rabbit on the run,
Tick-tock, and here comes the fun.
What's under that rock, oh bother?
A gummy bear or just our father?

The unknown smiles, a mischievous friend,
With every twist, there lies a bend.
In the kaleidoscope of dazzling sights,
We find glee in the cosmic fights.

The Humor in Heartbeats

With every thump, the heart beats loud,
A drummer's band in a bustling crowd.
What's the rhythm to this life we play?
A comedy show, come what may.

Tickled pink, the pulse races high,
Hearts wear capes as they swirl and fly.
Each beat a-echoing laughter's ring,
Who says absurdity can't bring bling?

Fingers snap to the silly show,
Winks and nods, a rhythmic flow.
What's love? A riddle wrapped in fun,
A dance of souls caught in one run.

So we sway, in sync with fate,
With each heartbeat, we celebrate.
Take a bow, let your worries cease,
In the humor of life, we find our peace.

Silliness in the Shadows of Doubt

In realms where brains collide and clash,

Curiosity prances, making a splash.

Why is a penguin not a potato?

Wonder stumbles soft on each weird motto.

With question marks floating in thin air,

Reason adds a quirky flair.

If trees could talk, what would they say?

A leaf might shout, "I'm off to play!"

Shadows giggle with silly weight,

Tickling minds that dance with fate.

Does the sun wear shades to keep it cool?

Or just play tricks on the wise old fool?

Cosmic Comedy: A Play of Existence

In the grand theater of vast unknowns,
Stars twinkle like friends with funny phones.
Why does a comet have a tail so long?
It's off to the party; the universe's song!

Planets hurry in a ballet of spins,
Each chasing laughter, where real fun begins.
If black holes hiccup, what do they eat?
Stardust snacks and memories sweet!

Galaxies swirl in a waltz of time,
Gravity's joke could be cosmic rhyme.
What's the punchline to life's big show?
Maybe it's just a grand cosmic "whoa!"

Delights in the Depths of Being

In the ocean's depth, where thoughts go to play,

Dolphins giggle, guiding the way.

How deep could wisdom truly dive?

With each bubble, we feel so alive!

Coral reefs curl with laughter in hue,

Fish gossip in colors, bright and true.

Does a jellyfish giggle when it glides?

Or does it ponder where humor hides?

As waves dance high with a playful cheer,

Life's silly secrets seem far and near.

What makes the sea foam into a lace?

Maybe it's joy in a salty embrace!

The Jester in the Grand Design

In the cosmos' court, a jester arrives,

Spinning tales where whimsy thrives.

Why do we ponder the meaning of schemes?

Perhaps the answer's hidden in dreams!

With jest and chuckle, the stars align,

Even the galaxies sip on fine wine.

If atoms could dance, what would they do?

They'd twirl in a jig, just to amuse you!

In shadows of doubt, the jester winks,

Tossing riddles like playful pinks.

What's the key to existence's door?

Just a joke wrapped in cosmic lore!

Whispers of the Universe in Giggles

In the void we ponder fate,
A black hole blocks our dinner plate.
Where'd the socks go, what a crime!
Space-time bends, oh what a rhyme!

Asteroids dance in cosmic glee,
While comets cheer, 'Come join the spree!'
Stars wink like cheeky sprites at night,
We chase the glow, in pure delight.

Questions swirl on cosmic strings,
Do aliens play or wear gold rings?
We giggle at the things we seek,
A universe where all is bleak!

What's the meaning, is it true?
A taco's fate? A life anew?
With every joke the cosmos sings,
A symphony of crazy things.

Mirth Among the Stars

Twinkling laughter fills the air,
Do planets gossip; do they care?
Galaxies spin, their jokes take flight,
Who knew space could be so bright?

Shooting stars with silly hats,
Fashioned from old cosmic mats.
Orion sighs with giggles low,
At black holes pulling all the flow.

Wormholes twist and turn with grace,
Time travelers playing hide and chase.
What's the punchline? Who can tell?
As cosmic jesters ring the bell.

Hidden portals wrap in cheer,
"Get it?" they ask—what brings you here?
We share a laugh and float away,
In mirthful space, we choose to stay.

The Paradox of Puns

What comes first, the joke or thought?
In this riddle, we're all caught.
Time ticks on, will it unwind?
Or just smirk at the punchline's kind?

Riddles tumble through the dusk,
Drifting in a playful husk.
Puns collide like quarks in flight,
Causing giggles deep at night.

Why did the atom cross the road?
To split the punchline—oh dear, my code!
Quantum giggles flirt with fate,
A universe of jokes await.

Chapter one, a chuckle starts,
Where every story wiggles hearts.
So ponder deep, and share a grin,
In the realm of puns, it's always win!

Cosmic Quips and Quantum Giggles

Inside the void, a quip escapes,
As starlight shimmers, laughter shapes.
Why is silence so profound?
Because it knows what's all around!

Photon jokes zip through the dark,
Each one a gleeful little spark.
Do galaxies ever blush or beam?
If so, they're caught in a cosmic dream.

Twirling through time in a funny way,
We chase the stars and dance away.
What's warp-speed but a comical spree?
Just another riddle from infinity!

Echoes of laughter spin and twirl,
The universe pipes up—what a whirl!
We're stardust, grinning, in this grand show,
With cosmic quips, let's steal the glow.

Jests About the Journey

Why do we chase the stars so bright?
When they twinkle, they mock our plight.
Maps don't show the paths of dreams,
Just detours full of silly schemes.

In life's great quest, we lose our way,
With every step, we start to sway.
But oh, the fun of tripping high,
It's better than a solemn sigh.

Through valleys deep and mountains tall,
We stumble, giggle, rise, and fall.
Each twist and turn, a chance to play,
With joy in hand, we dance away.

So here's to paths we do not know,
With laughter's spark, our spirits grow.
In every hiccup, there's a cheer,
The jest of life is always near.

The Joyful Enigma

What's the purpose? Shouted from the crowd,
Yet silence answers, clear and loud.
We ponder hard with puzzled eyes,
While giggles bubble, what a surprise!

The riddle spins, and so do we,
In circles round, so wild and free.
With each "why" echoing in the air,
We find more joy than we could bear.

Clocks tick softly, they mock the wise,
As laughter bubbles, we don our disguise.
A dance of thoughts, a playful tease,
Life's grand puzzle, a jester's breeze.

So join the fun, release the fret,
In every question, joy is set.
With a wink at fate, we jest along,
In this delightful, silly song.

Humor in the Heart of the Void

In the vastness where the stars collide,
We hop on comets, take a ride.
What's out there? A cosmic jest,
Where questions swirl, we're all a guest.

With each black hole, we grin and sway,
As mysteries dance and play all day.
In the grip of uncertainty's weave,
We chuckle softly, "What do we believe?"

Gravity tugs, and we lose our grip,
But laughter's rocket gives us the trip.
In empty space, we fill with cheer,
For the void just whispers, "Have no fear."

So here we float, with humor's light,
In the depths of wonder, we take flight.
With every bind, we giggle and shine,
For in the unknown, we sip the divine.

Snickers in the Silence

In the quiet where thoughts collide,
A chuckle escapes, we cannot hide.
What's silence saying, a secret code?
Whispers of joy, our laughter flowed.

With every pause, we find a grin,
As answers dance on a whim.
A smirk at fate, we take our stand,
In the stillness, we craft our brand.

Each heavy thought, a feather dropped,
In the hush, our worries stopped.
With light hearts we march along,
In the silence, we sing our song.

So let the stillness hold its sway,
We'll snicker at what's gone astray.
For in each moment of sweet retreat,
Laughter waits, a tasty treat.

Wit and Wonder Under the Moon

Under the night's soft glow,
Stars twinkle like they know.
Why's the sky so very high?
Ask a cloud, it just floats by.

Philosophers gaze, pens in hand,
Can they grasp what they don't understand?
Cats ponder life on a fence,
While dogs chase tails, it makes no sense.

The moon winks, a secret to share,
Is it cheese or did I dare?
Grinning, I dance with shadows of trees,
What's the fuss, just let it be!

In this cosmic comedy, all is light,
Giggles echo into the night.
Laughter spills from my heart so free,
In wonder, the world feels like glee.

An Ode to Cosmic Humor

In the vastness of the skies,
Even comets have their sighs.
Why do meteors fall like stars?
Perhaps just testing their fast cars.

Planets spin in their great dance,
Making time curve, oh what a chance!
The sun chuckles, warming the day,
While Saturn's rings twirl and sway.

Asteroids crash with a playful thud,
Creating craters, here lies the dud.
What's the point of all this space?
Maybe it's just a limitless race.

So let's toast to the stars so bright,
With cosmic punch on a moonlit night.
In the universe's jest lies a cheer,
For questions that tickle, never fear!

Grinning Grains of Sand

On the beach where time stands still,
Grains of sand with tales to spill.
What's the meaning of the sea?
A giant's tear? Or just for me?

Seagulls squawk their witty truths,
Chasing waves with playful sleuths.
Is the tide a dancer, bold and free?
Or a choreographed mystery?

Footprints vanish, the tide rolls in,
Like lost thoughts that never begin.
Why do oceans kiss the shore?
It's their secret, forevermore.

So let's splash in the salty foam,
Where laughter finds its airy home.
In grains of sand, we see the fun,
A beachside riddle for everyone.

Chortles in the Chaos

In the whirlwind of life's great spin,
Chaos reigns but don't give in.
Why does a chicken cross the road?
To dodge the jokes that overflowed!

Traffic jams play a funny tune,
As cars honk their verse to the moon.
What's the rush, can we not see?
Life's a comedy, a grand spree.

Rain clouds gather, plotting their wars,
Only to water a garden of puns and scores.
Can life's mess turn to a dance?
It's all about taking the chance!

So when the world flips and scrambles,
Embrace the giggles, laugh at the rambles.
In the chaos, we find our cheer,
With chortles loud enough to hear!

Jocular Journeys Through Milky Ways

We ride our ships on stardust streams,
Exploring all our cosmic dreams.
Planets flicker, they say, 'Hello!'
While comets dash with a playful glow.

Why ponder things too deep or vast?
A quark might just be first and last.
With galaxies that wink and sway,
We giggle through the Milky Way.

Space dust dances, a waltz so bright,
While moons engage in a powder fight.
The stars chuckle with a gleeful tease,
As we chase light on an astral breeze.

So pack your jokes in a rocket's hold,
And trade your worries for dreams retold.
In this vastness, let joy be the key,
For the universe loves a good comedy.

Banter on the Brink of Belief

At the edge of reason, we toss a coin,
Heads say 'yes' and tails annoy.
Is there a plan? Who even knows?
But the drama of life is what truly shows.

With every doubt, a giggle springs,
As theories flap like unwrapped wings.
The cosmos winks at our perplexed frown,
While we jest about falling down.

Jokes make the heavy questions light,
Even black holes genuflect in delight.
Who needs answers when we can jest,
On an existential rollercoaster quest?

So raise a toast to the puzzled minds,
To the fun in the truths that no one finds.
In this grand play, be it comedy or strife,
Let humor guide the riddle of life.

The Smile of Creation

In the garden of galaxies, we plant our glee,
Spouting laughter like seeds from a carefree tree.
Creation's sketch, a whimsical art,
With quirky stars playing every part.

As physics spins with a playful grace,
We whirl around in this brilliant space.
The cosmos giggles at our confused plight,
Beneath constellations that shimmer and bite.

Here's a truth that's silly but bright:
Even the void has a sense of light.
With every quirk, we make it a game,
In the smile of creation, no two are the same.

So let's frolic in theories that sway,
In the joyous dance of a cosmic ballet.
For if we ponder, let it be with cheer,
Each smile of stardust wipes away the fear.

Cosmic Banter in the Dark

In the quiet of night, stars hatch a plot,
Chortling softly in a cosmos hot.
What's a galaxy but a jesting crew?
With hiccups of light and twinkling dew.

Under the moon's cheeky, silver grin,
We flip through questions, let the fun begin.
Why take it heavy when laughter's the spark?
Even the shadows know how to quark!

Nebulas swirl in their paintbrush play,
Whispering punchlines in a nebula ballet.
Orbits spin like dervishes free,
While black holes chuckle at our curiosity.

So gather the jokes from the cosmic shelf,
And tickle your thoughts with laughter yourself.
For in the endless vastness, tells a tale,
Where humor reigns, and we shall not fail.

Grinning at the Great Unknown

Why do we wonder what lies beyond?
Stars tickle our minds, we chuckle, we respond.
Questions like clouds float, swirling up high,
Where do we go when we wave goodbye?

Atoms may dance in a cosmic play,
Yet we insist on puzzling the day.
With giggles about fate's mysterious schemes,
Life's a riddle wrapped up in dreams.

What's the secret that rivers can tell?
Why does the moon keep flirting so well?
A riddle of cheese in the galaxy vast,
Answers that waltz in a whimsical cast.

So we grin at the mysteries not yet unspooled,
Giving a wink as the cosmos is ruled.
For in every question, there's humor to find,
A dance with the unknown, we're cleverly blind.

A Lighthearted Look at Eternity

Is forever just a really long wait?
A cosmic joke at the hands of fate?
Time's a fella with a mischievous grin,
Saying, "Just one more riddle, let's spin!"

A tick on the clock, is it ticking for fun?
Each second a sneeze, a little 'achoo' run.
We'll chase infinity with ice cream in hand,
In a delightful search for a timeless land.

Paradise means knowing it's all just a play,
While angels take breaks for a coffee and say,
"Is it noon or is time just a clever disguise?"
In laughing at hours, the limits can fly.

So let's sip on the moments, with giggles and cheer,
As eternity whispers that it's nothing to fear.
For who needs the answers when joy is the key?
Eternity's punchline is all that we see.

The Universe's Punchline

What if stars burst forth with silly jokes?
A comet slips by, in giggles it pokes.
Planets with puns spinning round and around,
In orbits of laughter, joy is unbound.

Why are we here in this grand little mess?
As if atoms conspired to summon our stress.
Yet here we stand, with our quirks and our quirks,
In a cosmic jest of the universe's quirks.

Behind every quasar, a chuckle awaits,
Balancing chaos with eternal debates.
For in every meteor shower's delight,
Are the punchlines of life, shining ever so bright.

So gather your smiles, let your cheeks go round,
For the cosmos whispers its laughter profound.
In this grand show of stars, let's dance with a cheer,
The universe's punchline is finally here!

Tickling Time's Curves

Time is a jester, always on the run,
Playing peek-a-boo with the setting sun.
With each tick and tock, we tease it along,
Strumming on laughter, our favorite song.

Yesterday giggles at tomorrow's embrace,
While memories tumble, a wild roller race.
Those moments we cherished in fits of delight,
Are dancing through shadows, in soft, twinkling light.

Playing games of hopscotch on the sands of our mind,
Tickling time's curves, oh what a find!
For every odd second, a chance to explore,
A giggle, a heartbeat, for oh so much more.

So let's twirl through this zany parade,
With taffy-like time stretching, never to fade.
Each wrinkle a story, each moment a laugh,
Tickling time's curves, let's embrace the craft!

A Jest in the Abyss

In darkness deep, we trip and fall,
A cosmic joke, we hear it all.
Stars wink at us, a playful tease,
Are we the punchline? Oh, if you please!

A floating thought, a giggle's spark,
Who's steering this? Perhaps a lark.
With every query, we swirl and spin,
Searching for sense that's lost within.

In search of truth, we crack a grin,
What's truly real? Let the fun begin!
A riddle wrapped in space and time,
Is life a farce, or something sublime?

So here we dance on this tightrope paved,
With questions bold, we're all enslaved.
In cosmic jest, we're drawn to play,
For laughter's light can guide our way.

The Lightness of Existence

Balloons of thought, they float so high,
What's underfoot? Just questions spry!
A wink from fate, a dance so free,
Is truth a puzzle? Or just a spree?

The sun, it shines with a cheeky glow,
While pondering matters we'll never know.
With every stumble, we learn to sway,
In the grand parade, come what may!

Giggles echo through the universe bright,
As answers hide, just out of sight.
Existence winks, a playful tease,
Are we just marionettes on a breeze?

So let's embrace this whimsical ride,
As we chase the truth and laugh inside.
With each delight, our burdens slice,
In the lightness found, we roll the dice.

Grinning at the Grand Design

What's the point? Oh, what a laugh!
You dig for gold, you find a gaff.
In tangled webs of thought we twirl,
Is life a dance? Let's give it a whirl!

Questions spin like a dizzy flower,
What's genius thought, and what's mere power?
In this grand scheme, we play our part,
With chuckles wrapped around the heart.

A universe vast, yet we're so small,
In cosmic terms, do we know it all?
With queries bright, we tickle the fate,
Is the joke on us? Just contemplate!

So here we stand, with smiles to share,
In the mystery deep, we find our flair.
In every twist, a jest divine,
We're grinning wide at the grand design.

Comedic Conundrums

Why chase the stars when they just tease?
In cosmic chaos, we find our ease.
A riddle wrapped in sparkled fun,
Is every question just a pun?

In laughter's grip, we find our way,
As oddities glow in bright array.
With comedic twists, we stride so bold,
What's the meaning? Let's have a fold!

With every query, a punchline's wait,
Life's a stage, oh what a state!
As thoughts parade in silly lines,
Is wisdom found in gleeful signs?

So chuckle loud and grin so wide,
For in the jest, we take our ride.
In comedies grand, we find our cheer,
Amidst the puzzles, we persevere.

Tickle My Mind: A Universal Play

In a world so vast, we ponder and jest,
Why do we blink? Is there a test?
Stars giggle softly, a cosmic prank,
While we search for meaning in a riverbank.

With every tick of time, our hair turns gray,
Is wisdom just fables that some wise men say?
The universe chuckles, a game with no score,
As we dance through the chaos, forever wanting more.

Why do cats chase shadows, and dogs bark at clouds?
Nature's own comedy, drawing in crowds.
The mysteries linger, like socks in the wash,
We smile through the quirk, in this whimsical swash.

So tickle my mind with your fanciful lore,
Let's giggle at life, and what's in store.
For questions are puzzles, like a puzzle without ends,
In the theater of thought, where laughter transcends.

Chuckles in the Abyss

In the depths of the abyss, echoes a tease,
Are we just stardust, or cosmic cheese?
Galaxies twinkle, with a wink and a grin,
As they wonder if light years come wrapped in tin.

What if the moon really is just a light?
A giant bulb shining through the velvet night?
While philosophers fret, with furrowed brows,
The universe chuckles, and silently bows.

If time is a circle, are we all just fate?
Playing hopscotch with moments, it's hard to relate.
Yet in this vast void where humor is spun,
We find joy in the riddles, life's just begun.

So let's toast to the dark, with a giggle or two,
For in nothingness, we still make it through.
With every conundrum, let's dance and embrace,
Embrace the absurd, with a smile on our face.

The Humor of Existence

Life's an odd journey, with twists and with turns,
Why do we seek, what the universe spurns?
In the grandest of plays, we're players on stage,
With absurdity penned on each weathered page.

Why do we worry, when time's but a jest?
Are we all just actors, on life's quirky quest?
The universe chuckles while watching us scheme,
In a spiral of thoughts, like a wild, wacky dream.

Every grand question, a cheeky little riddle,
Are we just a folk tune, a whimsical fiddle?
As we tango with chaos, and jive through the fray,
The humor of existence keeps dullness at bay.

So let's toast to the absurd, with laughter in tow,
In this wild little dance, we all come to know.
Life's puzzle is funny, let's chuckle and cheer,
For the answers we seek are all nestled right here.

Jokes from Beyond the Veil

Whispers from shadows, they giggle and tease,
What's the meaning of life? Oh, please!
Beyond the veil, the spirits all play,
Making puns about how we bumble each day.

Is the afterlife bustling? Or just a nice snooze?
Do they roll dice, or sip cosmic blues?
Questions hang softly, like fog on the hill,
While the cosmos looks on, with a playful thrill.

If ghosts tell their stories, do they get a laugh?
Or is it just silence on that starry path?
In the grand joke of life, we're all in the mix,
With riddles and chuckles, like interstellar tricks.

So take a deep breath, as we wander the dark,
The punchline awaits, it's a celestial spark.
With humor as our guide, we'll never be lost,
For in the face of the void, we just laugh at the cost.

Reflections of Joy in the Void

In the depths of silence, I ponder,
Is this void a joke, or mere wonder?
Stars twinkle like they know the plan,
While I question if I'm really a man.

A cosmic riddle, all wrapped in light,
What's the punchline? It's quite a sight!
Galaxies giggle, they spin and dance,
Inviting me into their twinkling trance.

Do black holes chuckle, or just devour?
As I stand here, lost in the hour.
Time tickles, too, with its sneaky ways,
Filling my heart with whimsical rays.

So here's to the void, so vast and wide,
A mirror of joy, where laughter can hide.
In the silence, I find my muse,
As I float through the cosmic blues.

The Gleeful Gaze at Eternity

Eternity stretches like a cat in the sun,
Tickling my brain, oh what fun!
Is it endless, or just a long tease?
Wink at the universe, if you please.

Moments collide, chasing their tails,
Time whispers secrets, then lovingly fails.
The clock and I share a jolly dance,
As minutes prance by, lost in a trance.

Infinity smiles, a sly little chap,
With an infinity scarf wrapped 'round his lap.
What's forever, if not a jest?
I chuckle along, it's simply the best!

So raise a toast to this comical spree,
Where questions flop like a fish in the sea.
In the gaze of eternity's gaze, I see,
A mirror of joy that sets my heart free.

Cosmic Cracks and Smiles

In cosmic cracks, where stardust spills,
Lies laughter hidden in the big thrills.
A comet sneezes, a star blinks twice,
The universe giggles, oh isn't it nice?

Planets wobble in their playful spins,
While gravity grins, pulling us in.
Between the wonders of this vast plane,
Who knew the cosmos loved a good game?

Quasars are chuckling, they blink in delight,
As I burst into laughter, lost in the night.
"Why so serious?" the galaxies sing,
In this grand dance, I'm just a small thing.

So let's frolic among the celestial gleams,
And embrace all the joy tucked in our dreams.
With cosmic cracks showing smiles so wide,
The universe beckons, come take a ride!

Revelry at the Edge of Time

At the edge of time, I hear the chime,
A party of seconds, oh isn't it prime?
With each tick-tock, the revelers cheer,
Dancing on echoes, "Come join us here!"

Paradox frolics with its quirky stance,
While future and past engage in a dance.
What's tomorrow, if yesterday's a lark?
Tickled by moments that light up the dark.

Yesterday's jokes still echo today,
While future's punchlines hide playfully away.
Time is a jester, its tricks ever fine,
Inviting us all to sip on the divine.

So here's to the edge where laughter abounds,
In the merry-go-round of joy that surrounds.
With each glance at the clock, we can see,
The wonders of now, wild and free!

Silly Smiles Under Starlit Skies

Beneath the stars, we giggle wide,
The universe, a cosmic ride.
Why's the moon never late to shine?
Is it just waiting for a good line?

Planets dance in twinkling jest,
While comets pass a playful test.
If black holes have a secret stash,
Do they laugh when they make things crash?

So we ponder in joyful delight,
What if fish took flight at night?
Do they dream of diving through air?
Or is it just another wild dare?

With every question, a grin holds tight,
Big thoughts make for a silly night.
In the end, it's all a jest,
So let's toast to life and its quest!

Tickling the Infinite

Tickling the stars with a feather's touch,
The universe giggles, oh, isn't it too much?
What if gravity was just a big tease?
Pulling us back, but still, we ease.

Hidden in numbers, laughter awaits,
Infinite puzzles, tangled fates.
Why do we search for meaning and bliss?
Could it be found in a whimsical kiss?

Thoughts bounce like balls in a cosmic game,
Asking questions becomes our claim.
Is time just a trick or a jolly prank?
Leaving us giggling at the bottom of the tank?

In the dance of the quarks, joy is found,
With each little quirk, we spin around.
So let's tickle space and time and cheer,
For life's big mystery is oh-so-dear!

Riddles of Existence

Why do we wonder, why do we sigh?
Are we just ants in a big pie?
With riddles swirling, laughter ignites,
As we ponder our place in these starry nights.

Do fish think the liquid is all there is?
Or do they chuckle at our landbound fizz?
Existence unfolds in a playful array,
Tickling the senses, come out and play!

Questions like bubbles pop into the air,
With each little giggle, do we dare?
If the universe giggles with such might,
Perhaps life's merely a whimsical flight.

So let's ponder the silly, oh what a thrill,
In humor we find the answers that chill.
For every riddle that twists and bends,
We find it's laughter that always mends.

Chuckles Through Time

Time stretches like silly putty, oh dear,
Do clocks ever chuckle or shed a tear?
Seconds tick by with a wink and a grin,
As we trip through our moments, where do we begin?

If history's just a comic book scene,
What can we learn from the jester's routine?
From cavemen's fire to the tech that we wield,
Is life just a playground, with laughter revealed?

From ancient philosophers, who ponder the skies,
To wacky inventions that take us by surprise.
Through laughter, we see the world spin and sway,
While all of existence joins in the play.

So raise a toast to the quirks we encounter,
As we dance through the ages, our spirits they mount.
In chuckles through time, we find our sweet rhyme,
The best of life's puzzle is simply sublime!

Mirth in the Mysteries

What's the size of a thought, I wonder?
Is it big as a whale or light as a thunder?
Do trees tell secrets with branches that sway?
Or laugh in the wind at what humans say?

A cat's got nine lives, or so they say,
But do they get bored, or just lounge all day?
Are stars just the universe having a spree?
With twinkles for giggles, how pure can that be?

Why do we ponder on things so profound?
When socks go missing, is magic around?
Does time have a face, or is it just wheels?
Rolling in circles, it keeps all its deals!

Life's a great puzzle, a riddle so fun,
Where answers are hidden, but jokes have begun.
Let's toast with a cheer for the curious quest,
In the realms of the silly, we find our best!

Chuckling at Creation

If the cosmos was crafted by a jolly old sage,
Did he chuckle while wrinkling each page?
Did he paint every sunrise with bursts of delight?
Or trip on the moon while in mid-flight?

How do birds know just when to take flight?
Do they gather in circles for plans every night?
Or do they just wing it, no worries at all?
With feathers and flaps, they heed nature's call!

Do raindrops play hopscotch on rooftops so high?
As they bounce down to puddles with joyful sighs?
And when seasons change, do they throw a grand ball?
With winter in white, and spring's cheer for all!

Life's a grand scheme, a jest full of cheer,
Where wonders abound yet remain unclear.
So let's dance with the quirks that creation displays,
And giggle at riddles in whimsical ways!

The Gag of the Galaxy

In the vastness of space, who keeps score of the stars?
Is there a cosmic joke pulled on us from afar?
Do comets just giggle, their tails all aglow?
As planets do dawdle, with nowhere to go?

What if black holes are just vacuuming cheer?
Sucking in laughs from all galaxies near?
Does time play a prank, wrapping seconds like bows?
While we chase our tails, oblivious, like pros!

What's the recipe for a full moon's bright glare?
Is it just cheese melted with cosmic flair?
Are aliens laughing, their laughs echoing wide?
With a saucer of smiles as they take us in stride?

Let's wonder and ponder, while spinning in fun,
In a universe where the jokes are never done.
For the gags of the galaxy invite us to play,
And to cherish the whimsy that colors our day!

Giggles Among the Gloom

When clouds gather heavy, does the sun start to pout?
Or does it just chuckle, knowing it's not out?
Are shadows just playing, or hiding their faces?
In a dance with the light, they all join the races!

If rain brings the blues, but drops come in beats,
Do puddles rejoice, holding watery feats?
Does laughter dissolve in a summer's warm haze?
While the world spins around, in a giggly daze?

Do frowns on the street secretly crave a good grin?
Or is it the moody that just can't begin?
For in every heart, there's a flicker, a spark,
Ready to burst forth, igniting the dark!

So amidst the grey, let's twirl with the light,
Where giggles emerge from the gloom, oh so bright.
In the theater of life, we're all part of the show,
Joining in laughter, wherever we go!

Amusing the Infinite

In a universe vast, we stroll,
With stars like confetti, they roll.
As questions loom large, we grin,
Chasing the cosmic whirlwind spin.

Galaxies dance, with a wink and a twirl,
Each theory just makes our heads whirl.
Who needs the answer? Just enjoy the show,
As time and space steal the crescendo.

Philosophers scribble, scribble away,
While we trade our thoughts in a game of 'Whatay?'
For nowhere to go but round and round,
Who knew the abyss could tickle profound?

So let's raise a toast to the great unknown,
Where even the void has a sense of its own.
In laughter we find the secrets untold,
A punchline at heart, and a universe bold.

Snickers Beneath Celestial Bodies

Under the moonlight, we share our dreams,
While pondering life's baffling schemes.
Why do we exist? A joke, perhaps,
In a cosmic stage where humor maps.

Stars twinkle bright like playful jesters,
Sending us riddles, our cosmic testers.
What if black holes just want a hug?
And time is a stretchy, old, worn rug?

Planets in motions, all dancing away,
Kept in check by a comical sway.
Jupiter grins while Saturn takes bets,
Trading secrets in distant silhouettes.

So let's giggle at galaxies wide,
With a wink to the night as our guide.
For deep in the chaos, joy still remains,
Throw your worries—let's catch them like trains!

Cosmic Comedy Club

Welcome, dear friends, to the cosmic show,
Where quasars and meteors put on a flow.
With laughter as currency, we pay our dues,
In a galaxy where the punchlines amuse.

Aliens chuckle in their flying saucers,
As Earthlings argue and toss their tossers.
"Is life a riddle or a cosmic prank?"
The stars reply, "Just sit back and thank!"

Every black hole a comedian's stage,
Pulling our thoughts in a whimsical cage.
So much uncertainty in comets' tails,
"Just wing it," they say, "And hope that it sails!"

Join us tonight for a lightyear of fun,
With cosmic jokes that weigh a ton.
In the laughter of stardust, we find and explore,
A universe rich with giggles galore.

The Wit of Wanderers

Wanderers roam through time and space,
With humor we wear like a warm embrace.
What do the stars—even they conspire?
A cosmic circus set to inspire.

Dancing between the what-ifs and hows,
We ponder the universe and make it our plows.
In the silence of space, our giggles echo,
As planets take bets on where they will go.

Questions hang thick like an old musty sock,
Yet with each step, we boldly unlock.
Is existence a trick or a whimsical tale?
With laughter as our breeze, we bravely sail.

So to all fellow travelers, lift up your cheer,
In the grand cosmic puzzle, let's persevere.
For behind every riddle lies joy to be found,
In the wit of our wanderings, we are forever unbound.

Finding Fun in Finitude

Life's a puzzle with pieces all wrong,
We giggle at fate all day long.
The clock ticks loud, but we still dance,
In this chaotic, silly, fleeting chance.

Questions hover like mischievous sprites,
We chase them away with our joyful fights.
Every 'why' becomes a playful jest,
In this funny little world, we manifest.

What's the meaning? Who really knows?
We wear our confusion like a fine set of clothes.
Together we tumble, together we sigh,
Finding zest in the answers that pass us by.

In the end, it's a cosmic prank,
We laugh till we're dizzy, then give thanks.
For in this finitude, we see the glow,
Of laughter, the brightest thing we know.

The Playful Dance of the Cosmos.

Stars waltz in the velvet sky,
They twirl and twinkle, oh my, oh my!
The universe giggles, what a sight,
As planets play tag, in cosmic flight.

What if time is just a joke?
A funny, rich tapestry, we invoke.
Wormholes bend in silly loops,
As galaxies swim like silly troops.

Comets are stardust, silly tricks,
They flash by quick, like cosmic flicks.
Every question floats like a balloon,
Popping with laughter, under the moon.

As we spin in our dance of glee,
We're just pieces of a cosmic spree.
With every chuckle, the stars align,
In this playful dance, all's well, divine.

The Cosmic Chuckle

In the grand expanse, we find our cheer,
The cosmos chuckles, it's crystal clear.
Galaxies swirl with a wink and a nudge,
While we ponder life, with a playful grudge.

What if we're stardust, lost in a game?
Every question's a joke, none are the same.
Einstein grins as time runs askew,
We stumble and fumble with a cosmic view.

Black holes are hiccups, oh what a mess,
Spitting out thoughts, just to jest.
What if tomorrow just isn't a thing?
With every 'why' that makes our hearts sing.

So here's to the giggles, the snorts and the sighs,
In this infinite jest, let's share the skies.
For in this grand play, through laughter we'll roam,
Forever we'll feel we've found our home.

Jesting with Infinity

Infinity stretches, what a wide space,
We frolic and stumble, our hearts in a race.
The questions loop like a rollercoaster ride,
We throw up our arms, with nothing to hide.

What if tomorrow is just a cliché?
Or today's troubles are merely ballet?
The absurdity tickles, it won't leave us be,
While we play with the cosmos, so wild and free.

Let's paint the void with laughter and cheer,
Each giggle echoes, it's music to hear.
Existential dread? It's a comedic plight,
We jest with the stars, shining so bright.

For life's just a riddle, wrapped in a prank,
With infinite paths, we explore every flank.
So let's jest with infinity, in a jubilant spree,
With laughter as our guide, we'll always be free.

The Humor of the Unknown

In a world that's veiled in gray,
We ponder life in a twisted way,
Why are socks always mismatched?
Perhaps the dryer's a hidden hatch.

Why do we question the vast skies?
When ducks seem to have no alibis,
What is the taste of the moon's cheese?
Maybe it's just fondue on the breeze.

The universe winks through its text,
Telling secrets we haven't guessed,
Is time an illusion or a game?
We chuckle, it's all just the same.

Philosophers ponder with great flair,
But humor's the truth we all can share,
In every riddle that time creates,
A giggle dances, and love awaits.

Jokes in the Void

In the silence of space, stars quip,
Comets giggle, and planets skip,
What's the weight of a shooting star?
It floats on dreams, near and far.

Galaxies twirl in a cosmic jest,
Who knew the void could bring the best?
Why does time feel like slippery soap?
Because it giggles through every hope.

A black hole sighs, it can't hold a tune,
While meteors sing of a cartoon moon,
What if gravity's just a playful friend?
Holding us close, around the bend.

As we dance on the edge of the vast,
In jest, the future and present are cast,
Join the bounce of the cosmic ballet,
Where laughter blossoms, come what may.

Grinning with Gravity

Why do we fall when our minds take flight?
Can thoughts be heavy as they take their height?
When we trip in the park, is laughter the clue?
That gravity's grin is winking at you.

Why do we ponder the style of a tree?
Does it sway just to chuckle at me?
We question the breeze that tickles our skin,
While gravity's giggle keeps drawing us in.

What if we float on a feather's soft breath?
All worries dissolve, no thought of death,
Is the cosmos just playing a game of charades?
While laughter erupts and joy evades.

Bouncing through life in the play of the now,
We tumble and grin, we take our bow,
When questions weigh heavy, we give them a spin,
For joy lies in giggles we wrap our lives in.

The Joy of the Absurd

In a circus of thoughts where we all collide,
Absurdity reigns, there's nowhere to hide,
Why do we search for meaning so grand?
When life's just a show with no fixed stand?

A chicken's crossed roads without any care,
For laughter's the answer that fills the air,
What's the sound of one hand clapping?
Just a chuckle that keeps us wrapping.

What if all answers are wrapped in a jest?
Each riddle a punchline, just a light test,
With every twist and turn that we make,
We find joy in absurdity, our hearts awake.

So let's dance in the rain, wear hats that don't fit,
Find joy in the places that seem to be split,
For questions that baffle are just ways to bloom,
In the garden of laughter, we find our room.

Guffaws at the Great Beyond

Why is the sky so blue today?
Maybe it's just feeling gay!
Stars twinkle like they just got paid,
Winking at the plans we made.

What's the meaning of all this fuss?
Is it just us talking to dust?
Is time a clock or just a game?
Tick-tock, it sure sounds lame!

If life's a joke, who wrote the script?
A cosmic clown with a funny quip!
The universe burps, and galaxies spin,
We're the punchline, so let's dive in!

In the grand show, we dance and play,
Can't wait for the next big display!
Serious faces just won't do,
We'll paint the stars in shades of blue!

Jest and the Journey

On a quest for the meaning found,
I tripped over wisdom on the ground.
It told me jokes with a cosmic grin,
Said laughter's the key; now let's begin!

Who needs answers when you've got fun?
Life's a ride; we've barely begun!
Questions rain like confetti bright,
Let's twirl and dance into the night.

A philosopher stumbles with a drink,
Says, 'What if we don't even think?'
With every sip, the truth starts to bend,
Why chase answers when joy's the trend?

So raise a toast to silly things,
To absurd thoughts and the joy it brings!
Traveling this path with a grin so wide,
Let's take a chance, no need to hide!

Chuckling Through the Cosmos

As we drift through this cosmic stew,
Are we mere dust or something new?
Galaxies laugh at our tiny plight,
"Who knew humans could be so light?"

Black holes joke, 'We're quite the catch!'
"Time's just a loop; we're here to stretch!"
Supernovae burst with a chuckle so bright,
"Creating stars is our favorite rite!"

Planets spin in a waltz divine,
"Join our dance, it's simply fine!"
We join the quasar's fleeting jest,
Find bliss in the chaos, forget the rest!

So let's orbit in carefree play,
Floating where stardust and fun hold sway.
In the vastness where laughter is king,
We'll join the cosmos and hear them sing!

Snickers in the Starlight

Underneath the twinkling skies,
We ponder life with goofy sighs.
What's the deal with gravity's clutch?
Is it just to keep us from too much?

Why do we worry, fret, and frown,
When bliss is just a giggle down?
The universe holds its breath once more,
As meteors race and laughter soars.

Galactic highways filled with glee,
Counting stars, just you and me.
If space is vast and nothing's real,
Let's dance a jig; let joy be our meal!

So here we float on this joyous ride,
Shooting for fun, so let's not hide.
In this grand tale, be quirky and free,
Join the snickers of eternity!

The Lightness of Being

What if the stars just wanted to chat?
Do they ponder if we look like a gnat?
Floating on dreams, we trip on our shoes,
Giggles escape, what else can we choose?

In the depths of the night, do clouds hold a grudge?
Or do they conspire to give us a nudge?
With comets as friends, we dance through the dark,
And sometimes get lost, but we make our own spark.

Do fish in the sea ever ponder the sky?
Can waves crack a joke that makes dolphins cry?
Flip-flopping thoughts in a whirlpool of gleam,
We float on the surface, lost in a dream.

So let's toast with moonbeams, shake hands with the sun,
Each gigglesome thought—an unending fun.
In this joyous ballet of questions and play,
We wonder if answers are just in the sway.

Cosmic Smiles on the Edge

What if the universe wears out its socks?
Could black holes just be cosmic paradox?
Planets in sweaters, all spinning with style,
Tickle the nebulae, just for a smile.

Do aliens giggle at our silly ways?
Or watch us trip over our clumsy displays?
While sipping on stardust in bright, whirling rings,
They chuckle at life's most bewildering things.

Picture a comet with glittery trails,
Zooming through space with its whimsical tales.
Does Time ever stumble, can laughter rewind?
In this cosmic theater, joy's unconfined.

If laughter's the answer to all that's unknown,
Then let's dance among galaxies, not feel alone.
As asteroids tumble and galaxies twirl,
We find humor in chaos, like pearls in a swirl.

Wit in the Whirlwind

What if trees giggled when wind starts to blow?
And shadows play tricks wherever we go?
Clouds masquerading in whimsical shapes,
Tickling the sun with their fluffy escapes.

If time is a river, are clocks just for fun?
Do minutes feel silly when day becomes done?
As seconds pass by, do they whisper and tease?
Juggling the moment with effortless ease.

Could rain be just laughter bursting from skies?
As puddles reflect those mischievous eyes?
With raindrops as clowns on this bubbling stage,
We join in the jesting, no need for a page.

So let's tumble through life, with wit as our guide,
In this whirlwind of joy, let's take it in stride.
Every breath that we take is a chance to revel,
In laughter's embrace, we find our true level.

Tales of Ticklish Time

What if seconds tickled as they dashed on by?
Do they dance in the spotlight, kiss time goodbye?
Moments are magicians with tricks up their sleeves,
Spreading giggles and wonder among the leaves.

As clocks play their symphony, swinging in tune,
Do hours exchange winks beneath a sly moon?
Each tick is a giggle, each tock sings a song,
Reminding us softly that we all belong.

Do echoes hide laughter in valleys so steep?
Or do they just bounce, restless, no time for sleep?
Ticklish whispers of tales yet untold,
Awaiting brave souls to embrace joys bold.

Let's gather these moments, tuck them in our hearts,
For ticklish time's magic is where each day starts.
With a giggle or two, we'll chase shadows along,
Writing our stories in laughter and song.

The Absurdity of It All

Why do we ponder the stars?
They wink at us in delight.
Do fish ever wonder of land?
Or do they just swim through the night?

If socks go missing in dryers,
Are they off on grand quests?
Building a world beneath lint,
Where every foot simply rests?

Do chairs dream of being thrones?
Or is wood just wood at night?
The mysteries make us giggle,
As sanity takes flight.

Playful Prose in Proximity to Eternity

What's the sound of one hand clapping?
A perplexing thought for sure.
Yet I bet it holds a party,
With silence as the core.

When clouds turn into candy,
Do angels taste the rain?
Or do they wrap it in laughter,
And send it back again?

The universe hums a tune,
As planets dance in bliss.
Do they know they're just spinning?
Or do they find it pure bliss?

The Riddles of Reality

Are we simply bits of pixels,
In a game we cannot play?
Each choice a tiny riddle,
We solve in a quirky way.

If time is but a river,
Can you fish for yesterday?
What bait will catch the moments,
That danced and slipped away?

When life serves up a pickle,
Does it laugh or just get sour?
We munch upon its tangy tales,
And relish every hour.

Nonsense in the Nebula

Do stars throw spaghetti at night?
And hope it lands on Mars?
Or is it simply cosmic pasta,
Twirled in the dance of stars?

If comets turn to candy,
What flavor do they choose?
A sprinkle of stardust magic,
To tickle the cosmic blues?

In a black hole's deep embrace,
Do ideas swirl and spin?
Or are they lost in laughter,
To where our thoughts begin?

The Euphoria of Existence

In the dance of stars, we whirl and sway,
Life's absurdity shines in the fray.
Questioning choices, we chuckle and scoff,
While the universe giggles and coughs.

Why does the sun wear a bright, golden crown?
Perhaps it just likes to show off in town.
With every odd riddle, we share a deep sigh,
What if bananas are really just shy?

The moon winks down, a mischievous sprite,
Suggesting we frolic in the soft, silver light.
If life's a joke, then let's all play part,
Giggles and guffaws, oh, the joy in the heart!

So gather, my friends, as we puzzle and cheer,
The big questions tumble, but we laugh without fear.
For in this wild game of cosmic delight,
We find euphoria in the whimsical flight.

Spinning Jokes in the Cosmos

On the edge of the void, we toss our queries,
Spinning yarns like celestial fairies.
What gives the stars their dazzling hue?
Perhaps they binge-watch as we do too!

If planets could chat, oh the tales they'd weave,
Of comets with secrets that we can't believe.
Hurling our thoughts into the great unknown,
With a wink, the universe calls us its own.

In the realm of the silly, the profound takes flight,
Why do we fret over day and night?
Amidst the chaos, we jiggle and grin,
With each cosmic joke, we're destined to win!

So come raise a glass to the sky and the fun,
For life's just a jest, and we're all but one.
With laughter unbridled, we traverse the night,
Spinning jokes in the cosmos, a delightful sight.

Cackles of the Cosmic Call

In the dark, a whisper, a tickle from space,
The cosmos cackles with a comical grace.
Who knew black holes could be such a tease?
Swallowing stars like they're cosmic cheese!

Each planet, a jester with pranks to unfold,
As we chase the light, and the stories retold.
What if gravity's just a playful embrace?
Pulling us close in this vast, funny place?

Galaxies twirl like kids in a game,
With laughter that echoes, and never the same.
As we ponder our fate in the grand cosmic hall,
We find joy in the quirk of the universal call.

So we tiptoe on comets, with giggles and cheer,
For laughter is timeless, as we all drift near.
In the dance of existence under the stars' bright thrall,
We relish the moments, the cackles and all.

The Jest of Time's Tapestry

In the loom of existence, where threads intertwine,
Time tells a tale, both ludicrous and fine.
Why does the clock tick with such a grand flair?
Maybe it's trying to impress the air!

As days slip and slide like marbles on glass,
We find humor in moments that quickly do pass.
What's the rush, asks the clouds as they float,
With a wink and a laugh, in their fluffy white coat.

Tick tock goes the rhythm, but we dance along,
Finding jests in the seconds, in every sweet song.
For every great question that makes us feel small,
Has a wink in the answer, a laugh in it all.

So weave your own jest in this tapestry grand,
With colors of joy, and dreams unplanned.
For in the jest of time, we're all but a part,
Crafting our laughter, with love at the heart.

www.ingramcontent.com/pod-product-compliance
Lightning Source LLC
Chambersburg PA
CBHW051637160426
43209CB00004B/681